NATIONAL
GEOGRAPH

Who Lives Here?

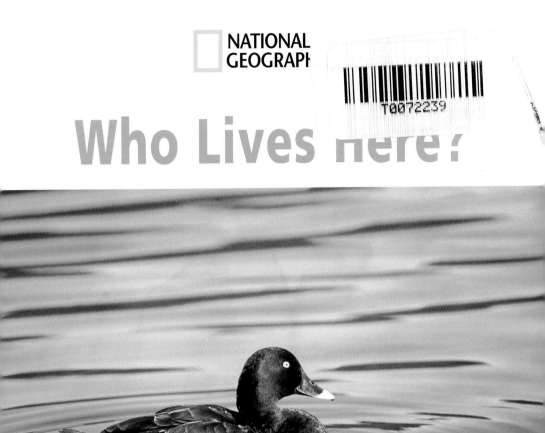

Sue Whiting

Who lives here?

3

A polar bear lives here.

Who lives here?

A crab lives here.

Who lives here?

11

A fox lives here.

Who lives here?

15

A duck lives here.

Who lives here?

19

A giraffe lives here.

Who lives here?

A whale lives here.